Bible R

A Study of Daniel

A CALL TO FAITHFULNESS

Pat Floyd

Abingdon Press / Nashville

A CALL TO FAITHFULNESS
A STUDY OF DANIEL

Copyright © 1997 by Cokesbury.
Abingdon Press edition published 2003.

All rights reserved.
No part of this work may be reproduced or transmitted in any form or by any means, electronic or mechanical, including photocopying and recording, or by any information storage or retrieval system, except as may be expressly permitted by the 1976 Copyright Act or in writing from the publisher. Requests for permission should be addressed in writing to Permissions Office, 201 Eighth Avenue, South, P.O. Box 801, Nashville, Tennessee 37202-0801, faxed to 615-749-6512, or e-mailed to permissions@abingdonpress.com.

Scripture quotations in this publication, unless otherwise indicated, are from the New Revised Standard Version of the Bible, copyrighted © 1989 by the Division of Christian Education of the National Council of the Churches of Christ in the United States of America, and are used by permission.

Lessons are based on the International Sunday School Lessons for Christian Teaching, copyright © 1994, by the Committee on the Uniform Series. Text excerpted from *Adult Bible Studies,* Fall 1997.

This book is printed on acid-free, elemental chlorine-free paper.

ISBN 0-687-02015-8

03 04 05 06 07 08 09 10 11 12—10 9 8 7 6 5 4 3 2 1
Manufactured in the United States of America.

Contents

1. *Refusing to Compromise* 5
2. *Victorious Faith* 14
3. *Weighed and Found Wanting* 23
4. *Is Prayer Worthwhile?* 31

Chapter One

REFUSING TO COMPROMISE

PURPOSE
To strengthen our resolve to be faithful

BIBLE PASSAGE
Daniel 1:3-5, 8-16

3 Then the king commanded his palace master Ashpenaz to bring some of the Israelites of the royal family and of the nobility, 4 young men without physical defect and handsome, versed in every branch of wisdom, endowed with knowledge and insight, and competent to serve in the king's palace; they were to be taught the literature and language of the Chaldeans. 5 The king assigned them a daily portion of the royal ration of food and wine. They were to be educated for three years, so that at the end of that time they could be stationed in the king's court. . . .

8 But Daniel resolved that he would not defile himself with the royal rations of food and wine; so he asked the palace master to allow him not to defile himself. 9 Now God allowed Daniel to receive favor and compassion from the palace master. 10 The palace master said to Daniel, "I am afraid of my lord the king; he has appointed your food and your drink. If he should see you in poorer condition than

the other young men of your own age, you would endanger my head with the king." 11 Then Daniel asked the guard whom the palace master had appointed over Daniel, Hananiah, Mishael, and Azariah: 12 "Please test your servants for ten days. Let us be given vegetables to eat and water to drink. 13 You can then compare our appearance with the appearance of the young men who eat the royal rations, and deal with your servants according to what you observe." 14 So he agreed to this proposal and tested them for ten days. 15 At the end of ten days it was observed that they appeared better and fatter than all the young men who had been eating the *royal rations*. 16 So the guard continued to withdraw their *royal rations* and the wine they were to drink, and gave them vegetables.

CORE VERSE
Daniel resolved that he would not defile himself with the royal rations of food and wine. (Daniel 1:8)

OUR NEED

Rarely does a week go by without the news media reporting stories of persons who have compromised offices they hold, businesses they represent, the public trust, their family and friends, and their own integrity. In contrast, under difficult circumstances, Daniel refused to compromise his identity as a Jew and his faithfulness to what he believed God required.

How do we as Christians most grievously compromise our identity and our faithfulness in serving God? We do so when we fail to live by the commandments Jesus said come first—love for God and love for our neighbors (Matthew 22:34-40). Our witness fails if our love fails.

When Christians harshly denounce other Christians or groups of Christians because of differences in belief or practice, the love of God is hidden from the world by their betrayal of it. John wrote, "Those who love God must love their brothers and sisters also" (1 John 4:21).

We also compromise our identity as Christians when we stop caring about those who suffer, those who are despised, those who do not receive the human love they need to be whole. Letting the world lead us into belittling others or into callousness is to compromise what is central to our faith.

What do you see as Christians' most serious compromises?

FAITHFUL LIVING

Daniel and his friends were part of the first deportation of Judahites taken into exile in Babylonia. Second Kings 24:10-17 tells the story. Although Daniel 1 quickly passes over the events that led to the young men's presence in Babylonia, we need to make an effort to imagine their situation in order better to appreciate the significance of the Book of Daniel.

In King Nebuchadnezzar's court the young exiles lived in comfort, perhaps even in luxury. But consider the grief and loss of being taken from your family, perhaps from a young woman you wanted to marry, your home, and your native land and having little assurance of ever seeing them again. Consider the loss of identity in your nation's being utterly defeated, its landmarks destroyed, and even your own name replaced by a name related to a foreign god. Consider the helplessness of living at the whim of an absolute monarch. Daniel faced this situation with no bitterness toward God for what had happened and no loss of trust. He determined to make the best of his situation and to remain faithful.

Like the king of Egypt in the time of Joseph, Nebuchadnezzar needed dream interpreters and sages. He hoped to find talented and useful men among the well-educated young exiles. They were to be taught for three years and then stationed at the court. The king assigned them daily portions of the royal food and wine.

Daniel determined not to defile himself with this rich fare. We are not certain of his reasons. Most likely, the food or the way it was prepared violated Jewish dietary laws. It may have been associated in some way with idolatry. Perhaps Daniel regarded the food as unhealthful, or he may have wanted to avoid being bound too closely by gifts and favors from the king. In any case, Daniel decided that he would not compromise his faith or his identity as a Jew.

Daniel's method of asserting the right to live by his convictions is worth noting. He respectfully asked the palace master from whom he had already received favor and compassion to allow him a different diet. The palace master gave an honest reply: He was afraid to countermand the king's order.

This refusal did not make Daniel hostile or defiant, and it did not discourage him. He went to the guard who had direct charge of him and his friends and proposed an experiment: Let us try our chosen diet for ten days, compare our condition with that of the young men eating the royal rations, then "deal with your servants according to what you observe" (Daniel 1:13). The results of the experiments showed the four young men healthier than all the rest. Furthermore, "to these four young men God gave knowledge and skill in every aspect of literature and wisdom; Daniel also had insight into all visions and dreams" (1:17).

For those who heard Daniel's story in Old Testament times, what significance would it have held? Certainly, the story testifies to God's presence and care even in the land of the enemy. It also testifies to the possibility of being faithful to God and to the way of life such faithfulness requires. Daniel took a great risk in asserting the right to be different, perhaps the risk of his life. But he made a great gain. He maintained his identity as a faithful Jew and retained his captors' respect and goodwill.

Daniel could easily have felt justified in enjoying any luxury available to him as compensation for his losses. He could easily have lost his identity little by little, failing to recognize how favors accepted were leading him away from the practice of his faith. Instead, Daniel became an example of wisdom and faithfulness that inspires others.

What are the "royal rations" that could stand in the way of your faithfulness?

SKIPPING CHURCH TO GO PLAY!

Traditions of Faithfulness

As Christians we are surrounded by a great cloud of faithful witnesses. One such witness was a barefoot Dominican friar, Antonino of Florence. In 1446, Antonino, at age fifty-seven, found himself in a place he did not want to be. In spite of his objection, he was entering the episcopal palace as the new Archbishop of Florence. Pope Eugenius IV had threatened excommunication if he refused the appointment.

When Antonino became archbishop, he had clear ideas about how Christians should live. He also knew the city he was to serve. Florence, under the rule of the Medicis, was the home of modern banking and a center of trade. Many people, however, had been driven into abject poverty by high taxes, forced loans, special levies, high interest rates, and high prices.

Antonino refused the "royal rations" that could have been his as Archbishop of Florence. He sent away those who had been enjoying the riches of the palace and kept just six persons to help in his work. He declared that the archbishop's "money, his time, and his powers" were at the service of his flock and began to minister to the whole city.

Refusing to Compromise / 9

Helping the poor was Antonino's first priority. He formed fraternities to raise and distribute funds for food, clothing, and housing and to make sure the funds were given in such a way that receiving them would not add to a loss of dignity for those ashamed of their poverty. He started municipal pawn shops where, for a small fee, persons could get credit to take them through hard times. He established homes for orphaned and abandoned children. He even dug up the lawns and flower beds of the episcopal palace and gave plots to the most destitute for growing vegetables.

Antonino also used his scholarship, his legal ability, his understanding of economics, his voice, his pen, and his office on behalf of both rich and poor. He was concerned for the rich because he believed the economic system that was producing a prosperous merchant class could also be an occasion for sin. In his view, "the first principle of economics is that riches are not an end in themselves, but a means to an end"—first, the support of oneself and one's family in a dignified but not luxurious manner; second, the relief of the poor; third, the furtherance of the common good.

In one conflict on behalf of the poor, the ruling *Signoria* threatened to depose Antonino. He replied that he would be glad to return to his friar's cell. That is where Cosimo de Medici found him when he came to beg him to return. Antonino served until his death at seventy. His will directed that all his possessions be given to the poor, but only four florins were found in his house. He had already given away everything else.[1]

Like Daniel, Antonino was not tempted by riches, power, or threats to his position in the world. He refused to compromise his faithfulness to God's calling. When he was not allowed to live out his days in the simple life he preferred, he made his new calling a testament to God's love and justice and a blessing to all.

Who are the witnesses that inspire you to be faithful?

Being Faithful Today

Comfort, opportunities for advancement, and good fortune can be powerful tempters to compromise our identity as Christians—especially so if we are always among people just like ourselves. Having what others have and doing what others do can seem natural and our right. We can lose sight of other ways of thinking and acting and of God's claim on us on behalf of those in need. In C. S. Lewis's *Screwtape Letters,* the senior devil advises his nephew to steer the man he is tempting away from a church that "brings people of different classes and psychology together in the kind of unity the Enemy [God] desires"[2] and into a church where everyone is alike, a church that is like a club.

Good fortune can also be an opportunity for living faithfully, however. I know a husband and wife, both excellent lawyers, who decided early on that money and prestige, which were easily within their grasp, would not be their priorities. Instead, they wanted to devote time to their children, to their church, to their community, and to each other. They were content with a modest home in an older neighborhood and needed no material symbols of success. They have given great riches of time, wisdom, humor, and love to their children, their church, their city, and their friends.

Trouble of all kinds can test our faithfulness. Daniel in youth and Antonino in middle age found themselves in places they did not want to be. A great many persons in times of illness or in old age find themselves in places they had rather not be. Yet, in those places many have the courage, faith, and love to be powerful witnesses to faithful living.

Such a witness was my friend Claire Bate. She would have preferred to live in her home in Cleveland near the lake. After a leg amputation, however, it was necessary for her to move to Nashville to be near her daughter. Claire was rarely free from the pain of vascular disease and arthritis. She was

Don't allow others to steal your joy!

also hard of hearing. Yet she never abandoned her sense of humor, her trust in God, or her interest in others.

On coming to Nashville, Claire looked for ways she could continue to serve. She became part of the Upper Room and Edgehill prayer ministries. She sent cards and letters and made telephone calls to those who needed a friend. She visited others in nursing homes; and when she was hospitalized or in nursing care herself, she always took an interest in the people who served her.

Claire moved from Nashville to Tucson where she was at Life Care Center near her son. There she endured an amputation and the illness that ended her life. In spite of all her suffering, the staff at the Life Care Center remember her for her loving spirit, her wit, and her gift for remembering staff and volunteers. The director of the center referred to her as "elegant and a role model for me." Like Daniel, Claire was valiant and faithful.

God calls each of us to be faithful wherever we are in life—in joy and in suffering, on good days and on bad days. Therefore, we need God's guidance daily in order to be alert to the ways we are tempted to compromise our identity as Christians. We see before us—and within us—dishonesty and untruthfulness, self-seeking and greed, discontent and ingratitude for what God provides, and a failure to cherish each person and each creature as God's creation. Yet the world that can tempt us to be unfaithful is the world God loves and the world into which God sends us.

God does not send us into the world alone, however, or leave us to live our lives alone. We have God's Spirit present with us; and we are surrounded by a cloud of faithful witnesses, both here with us on earth and present with us in memory. God promises,

> I, the LORD your God,
>   hold your right hand;

it is I who say to you, "Do not fear,
I will help you."
(Isaiah 41:13)

What commitments do you want to make to live more faithfully as a servant of God

> GIVE ALL THAT I CAN, IN EVERY CALLING - KEEP EYE ON JESUS AND HIS LIFE & DEATH - LOVE ALL OTHERS -

> **CLOSING PRAYER**
> O God, we thank you for the faithful witnesses who surround us. Yet we know that we need your guidance and strength if we are to live as your faithful people. Give us the discernment to know your way and the will to follow it. Fill us with your Holy Spirit that we may be honest, just, and loving in all that we do. In Jesus' name we pray. Amen.

---

[1] From *The Radical Tradition: Revolutionary Saints in the Battle for Justice and Human Rights*, edited by Gilbert Márcus (Doubleday, 1992); pages 75–83.
[2] From *Screwtape Letters*, by C.S. Lewis (The Macmillan Company, 1944); page 81.

Chapter Two

VICTORIOUS FAITH

PURPOSE
To help us reflect on why we serve God

BIBLE PASSAGE
Daniel 3:14, 16-25

14 Nebuchadnezzar said to them, "Is it true, O Shadrach, Meschach, and Abednego, that you do not serve my gods and you do not worship the golden statue that I have set up?" . . .

16 Shadrach, Meshach, and Abednego answered the king, "O Nebuchadnezzar, we have no need to present a defense to you in this matter. 17 If our God whom we serve is able to deliver us from the furnace of blazing fire and out of your hand, O king, let him deliver us. 18 But if not, be it known to you, O king, that we will not serve your gods and we will not worship the golden statue that you have set up."

19 Then Nebuchadnezzar was so filled with rage against Shadrach, Meshach, and Abednego that his face was distorted. He ordered the furnace heated up seven times more than was customary, 20 and ordered some of the strongest guards in his army to bind Shadrach, Meshach, and Abednego and to throw them into the furnace of blazing fire. 21 So the

men were bound, still wearing their tunics, their trousers, their hats, and their other garments, and they were thrown in the furnace of blazing fire. 22 Because the king's command was urgent and the furnace was so overheated, the raging flames killed the men who lifted Shadrach, Meshach, and Abednego. 23 But the three men, Shadrach, Meshach, and Abednego, fell down, bound, into the furnace of blazing fire.

24 Then King Nebuchadnezzar was astonished and rose up quickly. He said to his counselors, "Was it not three men that we threw bound into the fire?" They answered the king, "True, O king." 25 He replied, "But I see four men unbound, walking in the middle of the fire, and they are not hurt; and the fourth has the appearance of a god."

CORE VERSE

Be it known to you, O king, that we will not serve your gods and we will not worship the golden statue that you have set up.
(Daniel 3:18)

OUR NEED

In *Spoon River Anthology,* Edgar Lee Masters lets the residents of the cemetery speak. For good or ill, those completely devoted to a single goal had often succeeded in that one thing.

When asked why they had risked their lives, many persons who rescued Jews during the Holocaust said, "I couldn't have lived with myself if I hadn't helped." Studies show most rescuers had reached out to others before the war and continued to do so afterward. What we decide and do day after day reveals what is important to us, but we may need a crisis to bring our priorities home.

Making a conscious commitment to whom or to what we

worship and serve gives life focus and provides direction for decisions and actions. Those who have a victorious faith are ready to say yes to God's call and to say no to all that betrays their worship of and service to God.

What would you identify as most important in your life?

CHRIST - CENTER OF LIFE!
YES TO SERVICE TO GOD & GODS PEOPLE
NO TO WORLDLY INFLUENCE -

FAITHFUL LIVING

Through Daniel's efforts his friends Shadrach, Meshach, and Abednego had been "appointed . . . over the affairs of the province of Babylon" (Daniel 2:49). Their appointment evidently made some of the Chaldeans jealous because they quickly found an opportunity to make trouble for the young Jews.

King Nebuchadnezzar had set up a golden statue (probably an obelisk, since it was about nine feet wide and ninety feet high) on the plain of Dura. He then issued an order that at "the sound of the horn, pipe, lyre, trigon, harp, drum, and entire musical ensemble, all the peoples, nations, and languages" should fall down and worship the golden statue (Daniel 3:7). Anyone failing to do so would "immediately be thrown into a furnace of blazing fire" (3:6).

We have no reason to think King Nebuchadnezzar was trying to make trouble for the Jews. His people worshiped many gods. Adding one more sacred object to bow down to would have been a small thing. However, Shadrach, Meshach, and Abednego served the God of heaven and earth who had commanded, "You shall have no other gods before me. You shall not make for yourself an idol. . . . You shall not bow down to them or worship them" (Exodus 20:3-5).

When Shadrach, Meschach, and Abednego did not bow to the golden statue, the Chaldeans went to King Nebuchadnezzar and said, "There are certain Jews whom you have appointed over the affairs of the province of Babylon: Shadrach,

Meshach, and Abednego. These pay no heed to you, O king. They do not serve your gods and they do not worship the golden statue that you have set up" (Daniel 3:12).

The king was furious! Still, when he called Shadrach, Meshach, and Abednego to him, he gave them a second chance to fall down and worship the statue. But he said, "If you do not worship, you shall immediately be thrown into a furnace of blazing fire, and who is the god that will deliver you out of my hands?" (Daniel 3:15).

Their reply is a model of victorious faith: "If our God whom we serve is able to deliver us from the furnace of blazing fire and out of your hand, O king, let him deliver us. But if not, be it known to you, O king, that we will not serve your gods and we will not worship the golden statue that you have set up" (Daniel 3:17-18).

They served God, not because they expected any advantage or favor and not because they expected God to rescue them from a horrible death. They served God because God alone is Lord. The One who created heaven and earth, who made a covenant with Israel, who delivered the people from slavery in Egypt, and who gave them the law was worthy of complete loyalty.

They worshiped and served God even though they had been taken to Babylonia as captives. Their worship did not depend on God's blessings.

The people of Le Chambon-sur-Lignon in France were like Shadrach, Meshach, and Abednego in doing what they believed God wanted them to do without regard for the consequences. They sheltered hundreds of Jews during World War II, stretching their meager resources and risking their own lives. A few gave their lives.

These people were French Protestants, Huguenots who had been persecuted themselves during much of their history. They felt a strong kinship with the Jews as people of the Book, and they saw Christianity as a faith to be lived out in deeds.

The people of Le Chambon had a strong sense of who they were and Whose they were. They refused to compromise their Christian values and faith when confronted with immoral laws. Furthermore, unlike much of Christian Europe, they refused to be bystanders when faced with great evil.

What stories of courage and faith inspire your actions?

MOTHER TERESA — SHE SAID YES — JOHN MCCAIN — GUARD MISSIONARIES — MARTYRS — CORRIE TEN BOOM — ROSA PARKS

Why Do We Serve God?

The purpose of this lesson is to help us reflect on why we serve God. We have heard the story of those whose loyalty to God was in no way dependent on God's favor or protection. Before we consider the end of their story, let's look at our own reasons for serving God. Here are questions to guide us:

—What do I believe about the meaning of life?
—What are my most firmly held convictions?
—What must I do if I am to keep on being myself?
—What must I say no to if I am to be myself?
—What do I believe about God?
—How do I serve God?
—What has shaped my beliefs about serving God?

I have never before asked myself these exact questions. I find I cannot conceive of the world or of life without God. For me, creation, my own life, and the existence of all things depend on God. Life continues because God sustains it. I have always lived among people who believed in God, and I share their belief. That fact reveals my circumstances in life as well as my own decisions. My sense of God's presence in prayer and worship and when I pause for reflection is a gift of God's grace to me.

I serve God because I am part of a history God has shaped. Like Shadrach, Meshach, and Abednego, my history includes God's mighty acts in Old Testament times. Mine also is the history of God present with us in Jesus Christ and God present through the centuries in the church and in the world.

In my teenage years I made a commitment to serve God. I have been learning what that commitment means ever since. Sometimes I fail, sometimes I am dead wrong, sometimes I sin. For one period of time I wanted to be disengaged, to take a vacation from everything. But often I grow and gain new insights, new direction, and a renewed commitment.

In serving God, I am sustained, corrected, confirmed, embraced, comforted, empowered, and inspired by the companionship and example of the communities of God's people who have accepted me as one of their own. Without the church, my service for God would probably be like the ember that goes out when separated from the fire.

My most compelling reason for serving God is my conviction that God made known in Jesus Christ a way of life that promises for me and for the world hope, love, and joy rather than despair. I believe God's love in Jesus Christ is a redeeming love for each one of us and for all creation and that every person is a loved and valued child of God. I also believe that God has the power to make all things new.

Even if God's power to create a new heaven and a new earth in which love prevails should be called into question, I still would worship and serve God. I cannot conceive of any better hope for humankind or any better life than serving the God revealed to us in Jesus. This is a life worth living.

Each person's reflections about serving God will have things in common with those of others but also things that are different. Hearing one another's experiences with appreciation and never with condemnation can enrich our understanding and strengthen our commitment.

In the final analysis, our reasons for serving God usually grow out of our beliefs about who God is and about who we are in relation to God. But we should not expect our answers to remain static, even in old age. God grants us the grace to keep on growing in love and understanding throughout our lives.

How have your reflections about serving God been helpful to you?

LOVING THE UNLOVEABLE

How Can We Trust God?

Although Shadrach, Meshach, and Abednego committed themselves to serve God and God alone whether they lived or died, God did deliver them. Furthermore, they were not alone in the fiery furnace. To his amazement, King Nebuchadnezzar saw four men in the furnace, unbound and unhurt; "and the fourth ha[d] the appearance of a god" (Daniel 3:25).

Nebuchadnezzar was overwhelmed and said, "Blessed be the God of Shadrach, Meshach, and Abednego, who has sent his angel and delivered his servants who trusted in him. They disobeyed the king's command and yielded up their bodies rather than serve and worship any god except their own God" (Daniel 3:28). Nebuchadnezzar was as impressed by their willingness to sacrifice themselves as he was by God's miraculous deliverance.

Scripture includes many accounts of God's deliverance from disaster and death. Yet we know that many of God's faithful servants have not been delivered from suffering and death. The prophets were persecuted. King Josiah fell at Megiddo. Stephen was stoned to death. The history of the church from the time of the apostles to the present has been marked by the persecution and death of faithful people. In our time millions died in the Holocaust. What then can we say about trust in God?

Even if God had not saved Shadrach, Meshach, and Abednego, their deaths would have had meaning because they remained faithful to what they believed was right. If they had bowed to the golden statue, they would have violated their own identity and their loyalty to God. Their lives, saved at such a cost, would have had little meaning.

Throughout most of World War II, Aart and Johtje Vos sheltered thirty-six Jews on their farm in the Netherlands. When Johtje's mother realized what they were doing, she reproached Johtje for putting her children in danger and for threatening them with the loss of their parents as well. Johtje replied, "We find it more important for our children to have parents who have done what they felt they had to do—even if it costs their lives. It will be better for them—even if we don't make it. They will know we did what we felt we had to do. This is better than if we first think of our safety."[1]

Those who trust God have an inner certainty, even though they may have no assurance that their own lives will be saved. Their faith testifies to the truth of God's promise, "I will be with you." God is present with us, even in the darkness of doubt and despair:

> If I make my bed in Sheol,
>   you are there . . .
> even there your hand shall lead me.
>   (Psalm 139:8b-10)

Those who act with courage and conviction witness to their faith that injustice, tyranny, and oppression will not have the last word, that in the end God will vindicate goodness, truth, and love. They can testify with Job,

> I know that my Redeemer lives,
> and that at the last he will
> stand upon the earth.
> (Job 19:25)

In times of persecution the Book of Daniel has been an encouragement to God's people to be faithful. It is an encouragement at all times to refuse to worship anything except God or to serve anything that violates God's call to justice, compassion, and peace.

How has your trust in God sustained you in times of temptation to be unfaithful?

CLOSING PRAYER

O God, make us steadfast in faithfulness, not looking to our own comfort and safety, but to your purposes for us and for your world. May our worship always be given to you alone and our service to those things that bring about justice and righteousness, mercy and love. May we be sustained by trust in your unfailing presence. In Jesus' name we pray. Amen.

---

[1] From *Conscience and Courage,* by Eva Fogelman (Doubleday, 1994); page 178.

Chapter Three

WEIGHED AND FOUND WANTING

PURPOSE
To remind us that God holds us responsible for our actions

BIBLE PASSAGE
Daniel 5:1-7, 25-28

1 King Belshazzar made a great festival for a thousand of his lords, and he was drinking wine in the presence of the thousand.

2 Under the influence of the wine, Belshazzar commanded that they bring in the vessels of gold and silver that his father Nebuchadnezzar had taken out of the temple in Jerusalem, so that the king and his lords, his wives, and his concubines might drink from them. 3 So they brought in the vessels of gold and silver that had been taken out of the temple, the house of God in Jerusalem, and the king and his lords, his wives, and his concubines drank from them. 4 They drank the wine and praised the gods of gold and silver, bronze, iron, wood, and stone.

5 Immediately the fingers of a human hand appeared and began writing on the plaster of the wall of the royal palace, next to the lampstand. The king was watching the hand as it wrote. 6 Then the king's face turned pale, and his thoughts

terrified him. His limbs gave way, and his knees knocked together. 7 The king cried aloud to bring in the enchanters, the Chaldeans, and the diviners; and the king said to the wise men of Babylon, "Whoever can read this writing and tell me its interpretation shall be clothed in purple, have a chain of gold around his neck, and rank third in the kingdom." . . .

25 "And this is the writing that was inscribed: MENE, MENE, TEKEL, and PARSIN. 26 This is the interpretation of the matter: MENE, God has numbered the days of your kingdom and brought it to an end; 27 TEKEL, you have been weighed on the scales and found wanting; 28 PERES, your kingdom is divided and given to the Medes and Persians."

> **CORE VERSE**
> *You have been weighed on the scales and found wanting.*
> *(Daniel 5:27)*

OUR NEED

Being weighed and found wanting is one of life's unpleasant experiences. Many of us can remember report cards or exams that showed us wanting in our study of a particular subject. I was clearly found wanting in seventh-grade softball. I rarely hit or caught a ball. In the unlikely event that I did either, I could not run fast or throw hard or accurately. Understandably, I was always chosen last by the unlucky team that had to take me.

Adult life has its share of being weighed and found wanting as well—the job we did not get or the job we lost, a marriage that failed, children for whose problems we feel responsible, a losing battle with addiction. Furthermore, we can be our own most severe critics when we fail to meet the expectations we have for ourselves.

Some adults have been weighed and found wanting in honesty and integrity, in their treatment of family and friends, in their responsibility to society, and in their choice of what they will live for. To come to full maturity or to old age and realize that one's life has been morally bankrupt or trivial or that it has caused others more pain than joy is a tragedy like the one Belshazzar faced.

In what ways have you been weighed and found wanting?

FAITHFUL LIVING

King Belshazzar had a great feast for his lords, wives, and concubines. Under the influence of wine, he sent for the sacred vessels King Nebuchadnezzar had taken from the Temple in Jerusalem. Not only did the whole company drink from the sacred vessels, they used them blasphemously to toast "the gods of gold and silver, bronze, iron, wood, and stone" (Daniel 5:4).

Unlike Belshazzar, King Nebuchadnezzar had come to respect and revere the God of the Jews (Daniel 4:37). Belshazzar showed no appreciation of the sacred and no fear of, reverence for, or responsibility to a higher power.

Yet Belshazzar's irreverence quickly changed to fear when he saw a disembodied hand write four words on the wall of the royal palace. He was terrified and sent for all the wise men of the court. Their total inability to understand or interpret the writing increased Belshazzar's terror.

At that point, the queen came into the banquet hall and said, "There is a man in your kingdom who is endowed with a spirit of the holy gods. In the days of your father he was found to have enlightenment, understanding, and wisdom like the wisdom of the gods" (Daniel 5:11). King Nebuchadnezzar had been dead for many years, and Daniel was evidently no longer known and valued at the court. But the queen said, "Now let Daniel be called, and he will give the interpretation" (5:12b).

When Daniel was brought in, King Belshazzar offered him the same rich gifts he had promised the other wise men. Daniel refused the gifts but said, "Nevertheless I will read the writing to the king and let him know the interpretation" (Daniel 5:17b). He reminded Belshazzar of how God had humbled King Nebuchadnezzar "until he learned that the Most High God has sovereignty over the kingdom of mortals, and sets over it whomever he will" (5:21b).

Daniel then described Belshazzar's sacrilege and said, "You have praised the gods of silver and gold, of bronze, iron, wood, and stone, which do not see or hear or know; but the God in whose power is your very breath, and to whom belong all your ways, you have not honored" (Daniel 5:23c-d).

Daniel went right to the heart of Belshazzar's tragedy. His attention was on gods who could not know him or speak to him, who could not give life.

How easy it is to give our attention to things that cannot give us life—a preoccupation with our own shortcomings, a sense of grievance for slights or wrongs, a critical spirit, the pursuit of possessions or of power. When our time and our thoughts are taken up by such things, we cannot be centered on God who sustains us and in whose hands are all our ways.

The Scriptures say that Belshazzar was under the influence of wine when he desecrated the Temple vessels. In God's judgment that did not excuse his actions. Yet in some of our courts lighter sentences are given for acts committed under the influence of alcohol than for the same acts committed when sober. Drunk or sober, the effects of violence against others are equally damaging; and such acts are more likely to be repeated by those who habitually relinquish responsibility for their actions. How can we honor God

when we are unable or unwilling to live as the responsible people God created us to be?
What lesser gods tempt you to serve them?

Your Days Are Numbered

Daniel told Belshazzar that God sent the hand that wrote on the wall. The people at the banquet would have recognized the words written. They could be read as nouns, the Aramaic spelling of the names of three coins—mina, shekel, and half-mina. They also sounded like past participles of three verbs—counted, weighed, and divided. To interpret the meaning of such a confusing inscription, however, was beyond human powers. The message was God's, and its interpretation was God's gift entrusted to Daniel.

The first message was "MENE, God has numbered the days of your kingdom and brought it to an end" (Daniel 5:26). This message was a clear statement that God's concern is with the whole world and that God's sovereignty extended beyond Palestine, even to mighty Babylonia.

This story became a message of hope for Jews who lived over three hundred years later under the harsh persecution of Antiochus IV Epiphanes, who desecrated the Temple and tried to wipe out their faith. The only hope for people living in such dire straits was the destruction of the established order. For those who believe in God's sovereignty, the fall of oppressors and the ending of persecution is a testimony that God created people to live together in justice, righteousness, and peace and that God's purposes will triumph in the end.

We also need to look soberly at our own society to see where injustice, discrimination, and suffering exist. Is our life together marred by prejudice and hatred? What is happening in health care, education, human services, and the justice system? Are we creating huge structures that remove a sense of community and mutual caring and responsibility?

Societies as well as individuals stand under God's judgment. Wise leaders and a wise people must always ask themselves, *Do our days deserve to be numbered and brought to an end? What things in our life need to end now, and what things need to have a beginning?* Our days are numbered; and, in many situations, our time to act in a beneficial way is limited.

Perhaps Belshazzar thought he would have plenty of time later in life to consider his relationship to the God of the Jews, but no more time was granted him. His time as a king was brought to an end because he was unworthy.

The appropriate response for us, as children of God, to life's brevity and uncertainty is to use time wisely and in a way that God can bless. I treasure a long visit from my mother several months before her death. But I wish I had written and called and visited more often during the months that followed her visit. As human beings we inevitably fall short in always using our time in a way that blesses our own lives and the lives of others.

How is God calling you to use this day and the days of the coming week?

Weighed and Found Wanting

The second word written on the wall was "TEKEL, you have been weighed on the scales and found wanting" (Daniel 5:27). Since the kingdom was being taken from him, Belshazzar had presumably been weighed and found wanting for the way he conducted his entire reign. We know nothing about that reign, but we can draw several conclusions from his actions on the night of the feast.

First, Belshazzar was willing to spend a lot of time and money in a frivolous way. Second, indulgence in wine was more important to him than the ability to act responsibly before his subjects. Third, he had no respect for what was sacred to others. Finally, the gods he chose to praise were purely material, having no lasting value and no power to enter into relationship with human beings.

Clearly, we are not weighed by human standards but by God's standards. For God, outward appearance is not what counts; the inner being, the whole person, is what matters. Jesus made clear in the Sermon on the Mount that anger, lust, and an unforgiving spirit are the roots of murder, adultery, and failure to love one's enemies. Jesus' teachings also make clear what God requires of human beings. We find the commandments: Love God with all your heart, soul, and mind; and love your neighbor as yourself (Matthew 23:34-40). We also discover in Jesus' life and teachings God's forgiving and redeeming love.

Reflecting on Belshazzar's story in light of Jesus' teachings leads me to believe that the sacred vessels being desecrated today are the lives of people created in God's image, members of God's family—children who are neglected and abused, those alone and sick whom no one cares for, those who are starving, those who have no way to make a living, those who are tortured and killed. Surely also the earth God has created and all its creatures are precious to God; to destroy them is to lack reverence for their Creator.

The final word on the wall was "PERES, your kingdom is divided and given to the Medes and Persians" (Daniel 5:28). That very night Belshazzar was killed, and the kingdom God had allowed him to rule was taken by another. Let us pray that we will be good stewards of what God entrusts to our care so that when we are weighed, we will be found to be God's good and faithful servants.

How have you experienced God's judgment and God's forgiveness?

CLOSING PRAYER

O God, we confess that every day we fall short of the example Jesus set for us. Forgive our failures to live together in righteousness, peace, and love. Open our lives to the love and grace you offer us each day. Open our hearts to our neighbors and our wills to the ways you call us to love and serve them, that we may be found to be your faithful servants. In Jesus' name we pray. Amen.

Chapter Four

IS PRAYER WORTHWHILE?

PURPOSE

To help us pray with confidence in God's mercy, God's faithfulness, and God's love for us

BIBLE PASSAGE

Daniel 9:3-6, 18-23

3 Then I turned to the Lord God, to seek an answer by prayer and supplication with fasting and sackcloth and ashes. 4 I prayed to the LORD my God and made confession, saying,

"Ah, Lord, great and awesome God, keeping covenant and steadfast love with those who love you and keep your commandments, 5 we have sinned and done wrong, acted wickedly and rebelled, turning aside from your commandments and ordinances. 6 We have not listened to your servants the prophets, who spoke in your name to our kings, our princes, and our ancestors, and to all the people of the land. . . .

18 "Incline your ear, O my God, and hear. Open your eyes and look at our desolation and the city that bears your name. We do not present our supplication before you on the ground of our righteousness, but on the ground of your

great mercies. 19 O Lord, hear; O Lord, forgive; O Lord, listen and act and do not delay! For your own sake, O my God, because your city and your people bear your name!"

20 While I was speaking, and was praying and confessing my sin and the sin of my people Israel, and presenting my supplication before the LORD my God on behalf of the holy mountain of my God— 21 while I was speaking in prayer, the man Gabriel, whom I had seen before in a vision, came to me in swift flight at the time of the evening sacrifice. 22 He came and said to me, "Daniel, I have now come out to give you wisdom and understanding. 23 At the beginning of your supplications a word went out, and I have come to declare it, for you are greatly beloved. So consider the word and understand the vision."

CORE VERSE
At the beginning of your supplications a word went out, and I have come to declare it, for you are greatly beloved.
(Daniel 9:23)

OUR NEED

Is prayer worthwhile? What would you say in answer to this question? How do your actions answer it through the ways you pray each day and in times of joy, sorrow, and crisis? through your prayers together with others in your church, in your family, and with friends? How does praying influence your feelings and understandings? your decisions? your relationships with other people and with God?

Human life with its sorrows and joys, its mysteries and dangers, its unpredictability from day to day, and its certainty of ending in death has led worshipers in most religions to practice prayer of some kind. Most religions look to a power that transcends this earthly life. We could say that if God had not spoken to human beings and invited our response, if God had not taken the initiative, we would probably have initiated prayer ourselves. Praying seems to be a human need and a human joy.

Yet when Christians talk honestly about prayer, most say that at times their prayers have felt empty or misguided; their sense of God's presence and direction has faltered; or they have not prayed because they felt unworthy or estranged or rebellious. We acknowledge with the spiritual that we are "standing in the need of prayer," and we confess that we always have room to grow in our understanding and practice of prayer.

One path to insight and growth is to discover how others have prayed, especially a person like Daniel whose life was centered in God.

How would you answer the question, Is prayer worthwhile?

FAITHFUL LIVING

Daniel, in his exile from a worshiping community, prayed alone. But his prayer (Daniel 9:4-19) is the kind of prayer we most often pray with others in congregations of God's people. Such prayers help us understand and profess what we believe about God and our relationship with God. They help us discern God's work in the world and how we need to respond.

Daniel had been considering Jeremiah's prophecy about the number of years Jerusalem would be desolate and the people of Israel would be in exile. The passage was quite likely Jeremiah 25:1-14. Verse 11 reads, "This whole land shall become a ruin and a waste, and these nations shall serve the king of Babylon seventy years."

Daniel did not expect to change what God had decreed, but he turned to God in prayer for help in relating what he had read to the faith he professed. Daniel's response to the Scriptures was a prayer of confession and intercession on behalf of his people. His fasting, sackcloth, and ashes show his mourning for the people and his attitude of humility and confession. His whole being was directed toward God.

Daniel prayed using traditional words and forms of prayer. He began by addressing God in words almost identical to those of Solomon (1 Kings 8:23) and Nehemiah (1:5): "Ah, Lord, great and awesome God, keeping covenant and steadfast love with those who love you and keep your commandments" (Daniel 9:4). His words describe how he understood God—as a great sovereign, as one who is faithful in keeping the covenant, whose love is dependable, and who expects obedience to his commandments.

Then in solidarity with his people, Daniel confessed their sin. He spoke of the suffering that sin had brought and of God's righteousness (Daniel 9:5-14). He prayed, "We have sinned and done wrong, acted wickedly and rebelled, turning aside from your commandments and ordinances" (9:5).

Daniel's prayer then moves to remembrance of how God kept the covenant and with steadfast love delivered the Hebrews from Egypt and how God allowed the people to be taken into exile because of their wickedness. In a similar way, we remember our history as God's people; what God has done for us in Jesus' life, death, and resurrection; and how Jesus gave us the Lord's Supper as a way of remembering him and joining with him and with one another in Holy Communion.

In his petition for his people, Daniel prayed, "We do not present our supplication before you on the ground of our righteousness, but on the ground of your great mercies" (Daniel 9:18c). Daniel's prayer ends, "O Lord, hear; O Lord, forgive; O Lord, listen and act and do not delay! For your own sake, O my God, because your city and your people bear your name!" (9:19).

Through prayer Daniel reaffirmed that, in spite of their sin, the people were still and always God's people. He prayed with confidence and urgency to a living God who had been actively involved in his people's history and whom he expected to be active still in the midst of the trials and tragedies of their life in exile.

What prayers of the church lead you to a deeper understanding of your faith?

Prayer in Our Lives

We know from the story of Daniel and the lions' den that Daniel prayed three times a day and that he did not let the threat of death interrupt his prayers (Daniel 6:10). I, too, need to turn to God at least three times a day; and my life is the worse for it when I do not pray. I am grateful that God is always ready to hear our smallest concerns as well as concerns that shape the fate of the world.

In prayer we can bring ourselves and our lives into God's presence to receive guidance, forgiveness, and blessings. But honesty is necessary. Since God knows us even better than we know ourselves, not praying honestly is absurd. But we may have the mistaken idea that prayer must be pious. Or we may not pray honestly because we want to avoid facing those things in ourselves that we wish were not there.

Persistence in prayer is as important as honesty. Jesus prayed often. He told the parable of the unjust judge to show his disciples "their need to pray always and not to lose heart" (Luke 18:1). Paul instructed the people of Thessalonica to "rejoice always, pray without ceasing, give thanks in all circumstances; for this is the will of God in Christ Jesus for you" (1 Thessalonians 5:16-18).

A good friend told me recently about his worst year. His wife divorced him, disrupting his life. He had to move to a small apartment, and his children no longer lived with him. He said two things saved him. One was a group of people from the church who came the first day he moved to show their continuing love for him and to paint his apartment to make it more cheerful.

The second saving force was prayer. He woke up very early every day and prayed, "Lord, I hate her. I wish something terrible would happen to her. I wish she would be hit by a truck. But, Lord, I know you love her and care for her just as much as you love me." After praying that way for a long time, he was finally able to pray, "Lord, help me see her as you see her and care for her as you care for her." At that moment, he said, the horrible burden of hatred was lifted from him with a blessed and life-giving release.

Sometimes prayer is the only adequate response to the events of our lives. A couple in our church have dedicated their home for God's use and welcomed and cared for many people with AIDS who were in the last weeks or months of their lives. One Sunday morning, just as he got to church, Al, who had cared for so many people, had a heart attack.

By Tuesday, we knew the damage to Al's heart and brain was so extensive he could not survive. At least two dozen people gathered around his bed when life support was removed. We prayed, giving thanks for Al's life and for the privilege of knowing him. We gave him back to God, confident in God's mercy and grace. We prayed for ourselves, for comfort in the loss of Al's physical presence among us. The love that filled us and surrounded us and joined us together did not take away our grief; but it filled us with joy and gratitude for one another, for God's gift of life and death, and for the assurance that God's steadfast love truly does endure forever.

Through prayer, we may come to know with our emotions and our whole being things we already acknowledge with our intellect. A number of years ago, I was lying awake, anxious and afraid. I did not believe I was praying; but my thoughts were, *God, I don't have any right to ask you for help because my own sinfulness has gotten me into this mess.* As I lay there, I felt myself held by loving arms; and I realized that I could not fall out of the grace of God. Nothing could stop God's love for me. I could turn my back on it, ignore it, and walk away from it; but God's love for me would still be there awaiting my acceptance.

While Daniel was still praying, the angel Gabriel, God's messenger, came to him and said, "Daniel, I have now come out to give you wisdom and understanding. At the beginning of your supplications a word went out, and I have come to declare it, for you are greatly beloved" (Daniel 9:22-23). I believe that when we pray, God will always give us wisdom and understanding and the assurance that we are greatly beloved.

When has God given you the assurance that you are greatly beloved?

Praying for Our World

Daniel was a virtuous man. Far from turning away from God's commandments, he risked the lions' den in order to obey them. Yet Daniel prayed, "We have not listened to your servants the prophets, who spoke in your name to our kings, our princes, and our ancestors, and to all the people of the land" (Daniel 9:6). Neither Daniel nor the young men taken into exile with him could have had a large part in refusing to listen to the prophets' message. Yet Daniel saw rightly that we are all part of the fabric of life and share responsibility for it, especially for the communities to which we belong.

If we build just, wise, and caring societies, we and our children will reap the positive results. If we do not, we and future generations will suffer. Our human condition has been so marked by sin that every generation has struggled with the results of their ancestors' sins as well as their own. Like Daniel and the prophets, we need to come to God in sorrow and contrition.

In our life together today as nation, community, and church, we desperately need confession. Too much public discourse is concerned with assigning blame to others and denying guilt, responsibility, or sorrow for the dilemmas we face. We all have done things we ought not to have done and, even more often, left undone things we ought to have done.

I heard about a young mother in public housing near my church who had finished a drug rehabilitation program. She wanted to stay off drugs, but drug dealers camped on her porch and beat her when she threatened to call the police. Her mother, who receives favors from the drug dealers, will not help her. She and her children are alone and helpless.

I do not know how to give real help to this young woman; but I have not even visited her to say I care, nor have I prayed for her very often. I confess that I do not want the pain of knowing about all the others like her in our city. And this is just the beginning of my sins of omission.

Considering the problems of our world in a spirit of prayer helps us see other people as dearly beloved by God. We are more willing to work together to heal brokenness rather than to become adversaries, each of us seeking to have our own way. When we pray, whether for an individual or about a problem the whole world faces, God often leads us to an understanding of what we can do or of how we can join with others to make a difference.

What needs of the world do you most often bring to God in prayer?

CLOSING PRAYER

Dear God, teach us to pray. You are present with us every day and every hour. Help us realize that you are seeking us even when we are not able to reach out to you. May we never forget that we are greatly beloved and that all your children are just as greatly loved as we. In Jesus' name we pray. Amen.